torse 3

torse 3 CHRISTOPHER MIDDLETON

Poems 1949–1961

Harcourt, Brace & World, Inc.
New York

FIRST PUBLISHED 1962

LIBRARY OF CONGRESS CATALOG CARD NUMBER: 62-9442

MADE AND PRINTED IN GREAT BRITAIN BY
WILLIAM CLOWES AND SONS, LIMITED, LONDON AND BECCLES

Definition

Torse[3].
[f.med.L.*torsus,-um,*
for L. *tortus* twisted.]
Geom. A developable surface;
a surface generated
by a moving straight line
which at every instant is turning,
in some plane or other through it,
about some point or other
in its length.

Shorter Oxford English Dictionary

ACKNOWLEDGEMENTS

Some of these poems have appeared in *Encounter*, *The Hudson Review*, *The New Statesman*, *Nine*, *The Observer*, *The Painter and Sculptor*, *The Paris Review*, *Poetry* (Chicago), *Springtime 3*, *The Times Literary Supplement*, *Tomorrow*, *Two Cities*. Acknowledgement is also made to the B.B.C.

CONTENTS

1

Seven Hunters	3
Amigos de Corazon	4
Objects at Brampton Ash	6
Oystercatchers	7
Metropolitan Song	8
At Porthcothan	9
An Alien Town	12
The Suspense	14
Britschgi, A Bookseller	15
Edward Lear in February	16
Yes, Mr. Brecht	17
Tanker	18
A Bunch of Grapes	19
The Guest	21
Aesthetics for Benetto Gulgo	22
Park	23
The Thousand Things	24
German Ex-PWs (Russia) at Münsterlager, 1948	25
The Hedgehog	26
Hotel Linde, Zürich-Oberstrass	27
Montagnola	28

Alba After Six Years 29
Flight into Egypt 30

2

HERMAN MOON'S HOURBOOK

Abasis 33
The Ant Sun 34
The Forenoon 35
The Dress 36
The Greenfly 37
The Sniff 38
Ode, on Contemplating Clapham Junction 39
Tenebrae 40
Waterloo Bridge 41
Pointed Boots 42

3

Male Torso 45
Southern Electric Teddygirl 47
Amiel 48
Absences 50
China Shop Vigil 51
Nightlabourer 52
Rhododendron Estranged in Twilight 54
Without Shoes 56
News from Norwood 58

Paganini 59
Matutinal Adventures of a Third Person Illustrating the Untold Agony of Habit 60
Cadgwith: 6 PM + 61
Climbing a Pebble 62
The Lake of Thun 63
Thinking of Hölderlin 64
Antiphon, After Laforgue's Stérilités 65
Glaucus 68
The King of the Chaldees 70
Thirst 71
The Lake of Zürich 72
Art Machine 73
Intrusions 75
Metropolitan Oratory 76
Five Psalms of Common Man 78

1

Seven Hunters

1

ON skins we scaled the snow wall,
seven hunters; roped, leaning
into claws of wind; we climbed,
wisely, for no fixed point.
There was no point we knew.

Staggered upon it at noon.
Drifts half buried it. The coils
horns eyes had to be hacked free.
We lashed, as the moon rose,
its black flesh to sledges.

It was dead as a doornail,
thank God. Labouring
the way down, by luck
we found a hut, beer and bread.

2

SOME came in cars, some barefoot,
some by air, some sprang from ships,
some tore in by local train,
some capered out of bed
and biked there with babies.

Like flies they filled the hot square.
The cordon, flung round that heap
of black tubes, when the eye blazed,
could not see. The crowd did.
Then we heard the first shout.

Now in our town the streets
and houses have gone.
Here, underground, we
who were seven are one.

3

Amigos de Corazon

HE's hard to make out, the old man next door.
All day he sits outside in his rocking chair,
Gap-toothed, in a blue shirt, and broken sandals.

About five times any day I pass him by;
He looks up from making his lobster baskets,
And smiles, but never finds anything to say.

He looks up and smiles, and nods his head
In a way that strikes me as having dignity.
He looks accustomed to tumultuous ovations;

But he isn't, he's like the goats hereabouts;
They're hobbled, but if you peer over their wall
And wait, they amble over to be amicable.

Sometimes this old gentleman takes a walk,
Around sundown, to the sea.
You notice he's not tall, on the contrary

He fits so well into the tiniest rowing boat
There could be room for something at his feet.
You wouldn't think it as he smiles over his basket.

One afternoon, a big new boat was being dragged
Out of the boat shed opposite. Quite a crowd
Had gathered; and how the people shoved and shouted.

The boat was so big two square feet of stone
Had to be hammered out of the boat shed doorway.
There the boat was, and everybody staring hard,

And the old man had run to the wall between
His dooryard and the street, and he was staring hard
And standing on tiptoe; and he had broken into a smile

That was different from any smile I ever got
As I passed him by, the usual five times a day,
Waiting for him to lift his head and nod.

Objects at Brampton Ash

THE quick thrush cocks his head,
bunching his pectorals, halted.

Long holly shadows hone his shining claw;
you thumb its edge and grass gets grassier.

The tapered spire, at anchor in its ring
of tomb and cedar, has to quit ascending.

So you revolve in hearth-smoke's occult caves,
banished by touch of frost beading the roofs.

What increase, could these ends outlast
perpetual waste.

Oystercatchers

So luminous around them lay the air,
The wavebeat died; rocks in the bay below
Retrieved their shadows, shrank to nothingness.
And here they flew, unerringly as souls; it seemed
The body's beauty died and they remembered
Only the dazzling wrists that launched them once.
In upward vertical flight,
Black M upon white M the wings' twin boomerangs
Fought the full blast of western ocean wind.
In level flight their voices rose like flutes,
And imposed on the air a sudden shape;
Short cries, unshaded, liquid, lingering
An instant overhead and then clean gone.
That black and white, by phantom definition
Anchored in emptiness, gave, almost one supposed,
Gave off the calm so luminous around them.
As bodies they could shed all trammeling,
More eager with their shape's precision move
For having mastered so their own harsh element,
Mastered the shrouding armies of the wind,
And launched in space another, wilder soug.

Metropolitan Song

ONCE it was wiser said,
Earth is by earth devoured:
Splendid day and the proud dead
Lie mouth to mouth.

Each work we undertake
Hardens to pistolshot
The heart we have to break,
But heart we have not.

Better we set our food
For the abandoned dog
Whose nighthowl echoes out
Of our deaf blood.

One morning more or less
Can neither curse nor bless
What time we leave,
Hasty to clock, in solitude.

Once it was other light
Prised up the shuttered lid
Ghostwise at midnight,
To drop our vision bread.

Once it was wiser said,
Earth is by earth devoured:
Splendid day and the proud dead
Lie mouth to mouth.

At Porthcothan

A SPECK of dark at low tide on the tideline,
It could not be identified as any known thing,
Until, as one approached, a neck was clear
(It is agreed that logs, or cans, are neckless),
And then a body, over which the neck stood
Curved like a questionmark, emerged
As oval, and the whole shape was crouching
Helpless in a small pool the sea had left.

The oval body, with green sheen as of pollen
Shading off into the black plumage, and the neck
Surmounted by the tiny wide-eyed head,
Were not without beauty. The head was moving,
So like a cobra it seemed rash to offer
An introductory finger to the long hooked bill
Stabbing the air. Danger had so
Sharpened what intelligence the bird possessed,
It seemed to pierce the mind of the observer.
In fact we were afraid, yes afraid of each other.

Finally though I picked it up and took it
To a quiet side-bay where dogs were rarer.
Here the shag sat, happy in the sun,
Perched on a slab of rock where a pool was,
In which I caught five fish for it
With a pocketknife, a handkerchief
And a plunging forefinger. But at six o'clock
It left the rock and waddled off seaward.

Though breakers came in high and curling
It straddled them, bouncing, buoyant,
Borne along the sealine sideways, with head up,
Slithering across the bay's whole width, and then
Drifted ashore again, to scuttle flapping
With webbed feet flat like a Saturday banker's
To shelter on a level rock. Here it studied,
With the air of one of whom something is expected,
The turbulent Atlantic slowly rising.
What could I do but leave it meditating?

Early next morning, on the bay's north side,
I found it cuddled under the cliff. The tide
Was low again. What hungry darkness
Had driven so the dark young shag to shelter?
It did not resist when I picked it up.
Something had squeezed the cobra out of it.

I took it to a cave where the sun shone in,
Then caught two fish. It opened one green eye,
And then another. But though I cut
The fish into portions, presenting these
To the bill's hooked tip, it only shook its head.
Noon came. The shag slept in the cave. At two
I hurried back. The shag was stone dead,
With its fine glossy head laid back a little
Over the left shoulder, and a few flies
Were pestering its throat and the fish scraps
Now unlikely to get eaten.

Ten minutes perhaps
I sat there, then carried it up the cliff path
And across the headland to a neighbouring cove
Where oystercatchers and hawks flew and far
Far below in loose heaps small timber lay, tickled
By a thin finger of sea. There I flung the shag,
For in some such place, I thought,
Such bodies best belong, far from bathers, among
The elements that compose and decompose them,
Unconscious, strange to freedom, but perceptible
Through narrow slits that score the skin of things.

Or perhaps (for I could not see the body falling)
A hand rose out of air and plucked the corpse
From its arc and took it, warm still,
To some safer place and concealed it there,
Quite unobtrusively, but sure, but sure.

An Alien Town

A VISITOR walked on tiptoe in an alien town;
Not that he was timid, but he wanted to see it all.
Curiosity, that was the point. And the town too,
Perhaps the town was curious about the visitor.

The noses were all familiar but unknown.
The horsemen in the squares also had noses.
These were known, but not at all familiar.
He thought: can one exist in such a place?

At night iron bells plundered the air with huge claws.
The weathervanes usually pointed southward.
From one rooftop you could see an old gold cockerel
Standing halfway up a mountain if the air cleared.
That happened when the weathervanes pointed northward.

Hollow bones and beaten bronze: everybody
Was hectically occupied, except the statues.
The suicide rate among adolescents indicated
That old folk only were permitted the dream, the dream
Backwards. Students were hearthbound, without prospect.
They grew old over interminable doctoral dissertations.

Gradually the familiar faces began to flush with
Hitherto unfamiliar terrors, a few home truths.
Regardless of their homeliness the unknown noses
Became the salient features of a savage landscape:
Twisted, tubular and hooked, lunar and cavernous,
With a lake of filth seething at the heart of it.

This was not, of course, the complete picture.
There were narrow streets smelling of fresh coffee;
Blue snow hills within a few hours' march; friends
Who knocked on the window to wish Good Morning.
Sunlight in the dusky squares, the scent of lime trees,
Even the brash blue trams were threads in the labyrinth.

That was the point. The town was curious, and
Curious about the visitor, in the sense that its
Elaborate workmanship pondered his moving image.
Might not the visitor have been identified with
That explorer of pools and streams who became a flower?

Familiarity from the start, this too should have
Posed the enigma, stopped the delusions at source.
Strange that psychology should have taken root
In this particular town, though not so strange

When you consider that psychology is the science
Of disengaging self from not-self; of confronting
Apparently ultimate masks with authentic faces:
That the patient may endure the invisibility he is.

The Suspense

'senza speme vivemo in disio',
Inferno, iv, 40.

You are too light, blonde, to bear much hardship.
Slight bones cannot carry much weight of weariness.
Bowed skin leaks, the long mouth voids a fountain;
Bitter as lemons then, your stocked heart shrivels.

How, fair frail body, can you pour out such holiness yet?
I mean this measure, being, where nothing was or shall;
I mean this body, grafting space to heal chained chaos.
Yours, the grave glance, belly's target, level smile:
You, pure injury to the poured blood, shouldering veins'
weight,
Base flesh you hoist up (how?) into the blue-peaked
eyelash.

Number may vanish there. Blind hence your levity brings
A calm of visions into the puckered face of things.
Even that world's elision into a wrung tear;
Even this radiance you wrench clear of the world.

Britschgi, A Bookseller

EQUINE the face, though first embroidered
by the delusion it bore that stamp of grace
fond Fotis once divined in Apuleius:

Wholesome the jawbone, jutting throatward,
cradles in eggshell brown a husky voice, the eyes
glint, are the haunted eyes of teraphim

Piercing abstruse disguise, and in the swim, bent
fierce upon discourse in clipped Babylonian:
of battered books and foxed, paper originals,

Of this one's foibles, the one they locked up,
of Benetto Gulgo, who dug undazzled for the exact gods,
and died of veronal: and this hoard,

Separate adventurers the usual market
chooses to spit at, their fortunate words
that tense his polyhedral place of office,

These black dawns he snared
with rounds of silver and made realities, all
his likely bread, have not increased his diameter,

Nor stature hunched by stoop, nor given squints;
for the ears are pointed a suggestion,
the eyes again slope almond, as if directing to the temples

Where (suspect as you may he is as tame as they make
them)
you will detect the new delusion (daedal, ineradicable)
of twin squat horns like thumbs.

Edward Lear in February

SINCE last September I've been trying to describe
two moonstone hills,
and an ochre mountain, by candlelight, behind.
But a lizard has been sick into the ink,
a cat keeps clawing at me, you should see my face,
I'm too intent to dodge.

Out of the corner of my eye,
an old man (he's putting almonds into a bag)
stoops in sunlight, closer than the hills.
But all the time these bats flick at me
and plop, like foetuses, all over the blotting paper.
Someone began playing a gong outside, once.
I liked that, it helped; but in a flash
neighbours were pelting him with their slippers and
things,
bits of coke and old railway timetables.

I have come unstuck in this cellar. Help.
Pacing up and down in my own shadow
has stopped me liking the weight it falls from.
That lizard looks like being sick again. The owls
have built a stinking nest on the Eighteenth Century.

So much for two moonstone hills,
ochre mountain, old man
cramming all those almonds into a bag.

Yes, Mr. Brecht

'Wie anstrengend es ist, böse zu sein',
Brecht, *Die Maske des Bösen*

A PERSIAN princess hangs on my wall.
In her white turban, robe of orange,
yellow slippers and white drainpipes,
I find her strange. She is alone.

A flower is in her left hand; with her right
she fingers the fan in her embroidered waistband.
On a slight hill, with deep blue sky behind,
she is musing. She may be in a paradise.

What slender symmetrical toes she too had,
that Indian girl long ago at the greengrocer's.
And even now, staring at such hopeless grace,
I have to fight to quench a yawn.

Tanker

SHE was built for the hard voyage,
tropical havoc. Rats chafe
her comet-coloured hulk, her shadow
is moored, her bells mute
as at matins. She was made
to forge through dry winds
hammering horizons and sperm
of the iron Atlantic's drowned.
And she is chained
inert in granite, enmeshed
by the engineers. Her spars
sag. Her dinining-room is deserted.
Only the whores
sway by wherever at high noon
Lascars tiptoe, spit,
and await orders.

A Bunch of Grapes

MICHELANGELO's Sybilla Delphica, upon what
  hard times wistfulness has fallen!
The faraway look is called a foolish thing,
  and even Rilke's girls may be lying all tousled and
tubby in bed, longing for lunch. Once though
  wistfulness meant knowing what others don't
but highly regard, seeing from a distance
  that something one contains cannot be touched.
So Goethe, coming into Italy, stopped a night
  by Lago di Garda, where he remarked
waves scrolled by south wind clutching the water
  exactly as Virgil had described them. And your
amberhaired unawakened girlchild playing
  in the park by water, in water, with a coloured ball,
was plumb constancy, in being precisely herself,
  not broken by oblivions of now and then.
Yet seeing from a distance that now and then
  can telescope, to magnify one instant into
a lilac light suffusing consciousness
  from its very ground of animal exhilaration—
this is wistfulness. One's world is multiplied,
  to share in what, the time before, was not itself,
or seemed not so. You best exist in things
  outside, are faraway, though they may not look it.
Wistfulness then is a luminous corrosive working
  through all immediate, objective, enveloping stuff
which has little or no regard for us. Suddenly
  you wake up, you swam like a fish in starlight,
and it meant what it was, the mountain pool,
  the balloon with a skin of gold that another child
hugged at your huge and crumpled bedside. And as now,
  in the panic instant, skimping responsibility,
even at wits' end, or just arranging for a journey,
  wistfulness remains, and puts the welter of things

for a time into order. It is a stillness
   nothing can sunder. It bears comparison
with a bunch of grapes on a plate on the table
   in a whitewashed room among wrinkled olive boughs
where the sun beats, and it is not yet time
   to be gone from that place.

The Guest

It's quiet, like this, by the river.
Fancy, there's a ferry boat without lights.
No barges here, no tugs or anything?

*

Bit of a draft coming up. It's like ice.
Plank's rickety. Quick, the torch. Now
Who in hell planted this nut down there?

*

I keep on coming back to your things.
The eye-trumpet. The speaking bottle.
This cauldron. Small brown Greek coins.

*

What's the long box upended in the larder?
Christ! But where've you hidden the bread?
Ask, man, don't just wait to be paid them!

*

You mean there's absolutely nothing to eat?
For the last time turn . . .
Turn those grinning . . . masks to the wall!

Aesthetics for Benetto Gulgo

(IN MEMORY OF EUGEN GOTTLOB WINKLER, 1912–36)

OLD men, forgotten, mumbling, all alone,
Must rage with visions, of dark dazzling skin;
Fair Helen's tumbled hair, her body pressed
Under their mouths, but soft, in shared surprise.

Husbands athirst, again, when the great noon slackens
Over church and garden, being only half aware
Their fruit is falling, begin to stare and tremble
At wishlike breasts on schoolchildren walking past.

Shall the face that shows no reason for disguise
Make dodderers forfeit wisdom and atone
For sins undone by going fast demented?

Is there such harm in dispossession, that we crawl
Backward through being, mindless, nothing done,
Heart-hollow drab, the whole house unfrequented?

This rose-dissolving wind, this doddering one,
Bequeathes a radiance, absence unconfined.

The line that breasts the form must be like steel,
Dread handling all we have that's beautiful.

Park

UNDER the walnut
They roundly cling
One cheek is all
Symmetrical
One mouth is hiding

The space their will explores
Has harsh perfection
Rapt from that realm at best
Where her shy breast
Shirks his protection

Faced with that free
Impervious place
By small degrees they slip
The yoke of see
The grasp of lip

But quick song warn
These malcontents
Draconic officers advance
With cordons whistling in
Suspended sentence

The Thousand Things

DRY vine leaves burn in an angle of the wall.
Dry vine leaves and a sheet of paper, overhung
by the green vine.
From an open grate in an angle of the wall
dry vine leaves and dead flies send smoke up
into the green vine where grape clusters go
ignored by lizards. Dry vine leaves
and a few dead flies on fire
and a Spanish toffee spat
into an angle of the wall
make a smell that calls to mind
the thousand things. Dead flies go,
paper curls and flares,
Spanish toffee sizzles and the smell
has soon gone over the wall.

A naked child jumps over the threshold,
waving a green spray of leaves of vine.

German Ex-PWs (Russia) at Münsterlager, 1948

SHADOWS mass, feet stamp the black earth,
Metallic sun
Streams down across the compound. Here they walk,
As if kneedeep in something. Where the roofs stretch,
Their eyes like thrushes' eyes flicker and hunt for shade.
Questioned, they suddenly shrink, timid, and blurt out
The stock responses.
Fluids rise from choked bends in the mind and coat
Their tongues with a bitterness. A heavy lid
Slams in the throat, bows head and shoulders, legs
Shaking. This prisoner has a penknife, opens it and sees
Seven winters uncongeal in the blade,
Sunrise of steel unhinge embracing armies.
Wan, he looks up, as if a door had opened and they said,
'Here is the land: we have come back to it.'
Only the knife is his. The transport is waiting.
When they embark, they wave their sleeves
With the levity of men who have ceased to live.

The Hedgehog

HOT March came with the hedgehog;
by the coal bin he crouched, first,
nibbling milk, mackereling
snoutmarks on the saucer's brim.
Then three successive nights he came;
came later the last night, dumped
glistening in the saucer
one small amorphous turd. Why?
In gratitude? We just laughed.
Scorn? Or some offence he took?
How hurt a hedgehog's feelings—
human he's not, though shut in
by belly and genitals,
like us,—or the isle untucked,
some blanket sliding off its
back, and he gone for he knew?
Southern wind this morning veered
crushing to cottage size high
cumulus and thicker grass,
warm as this child's hand, which tugs;
for Quick, she said, and Quick, Come,
and we found the path cracked, ants
rushed from the crack all around
the turd freshly planted there.
I think she knew the plain cause,
for Now! she said, then exclaimed:
Better not hurt these sweet ants!

Hotel Linde, Zürich-Oberstrass

FINKSLIN, mastercook and king of the Linde,
A man compact and hard of head, requires
For each fresh guest a white embroidered napkin,
A toast, for regulars, or a gesture of the hand.
In his soup may be perceived no fishbone.
Within his doors, the wine pours with a difference.

His combed helmet of silver has logic in it,
Roofs over smiles to goodevening various
Grotesques gathered for meat and talk at his tables.
Champions in skittles, Gygax the gallowbird,
Cannot bruise his aplomb. How calm, how warm
His consort comes annealing, to adorn his order!

Red beams aglow beneath fog in January;
Red lattice, blown loose, beat under wind;
Snow silted up all little lamps and orifices;
At six, frozen, beds divulge their bleary forms.

'Your bookcase you shall have. I have ordered it.'
He walks bolt upright when he walks upstairs.

Montagnola

A FAN with five peaks cools his door
in the hot hill. Forked paths lead there.
Under chestnut you pass caves for clear wine;
swerve over gradients of changing green;
float through woody dark following the bird-note
sung by two birds. His windowsill
showed white trousers; on the balcony
a lanky hawk stared and stooped. That afternoon
he stirred, with a silver spoon, his coffee backwards,
because of rheumatism; you could have sworn,
as he spoke to unspeak every word he spoke,
that his freedom was a way to deny nothing.
His only memorable remark was an afterthought:
a butterfly with open wings
clung alive to the minute-hand of his study clock.
He did not allude to his lyric on the subject;
and on reflection it was hard to tell if paradox
or wisdom lay, inextricably veiled,
in the churning limpid well of his senescence.

Alba After Six Years

THERE was a winter
            dark fell by five
four noses ran
            and shouting children
she got so quickly in a rage.

Now when I wake
            through mist and petrol
birdsong cannonades
            blaze open-sighted
at a climbing sun.

Hopeful but prone
            I turn to face a wall
between me and that wall
            surprised to meet
wild arms which did not hold this way before.

Flight Into Egypt

THEY saw them pass, the old man limping, the donkey,
The hooded woman, riding sidesaddle,
And the bundle she held as if it were valuable.
They heard the beast sigh, for sand scattering
Rose under wind as vision under an eyelid.
And the four went veiled
Into the dark which swallowed them up in Egypt.

Who had seen this could understand
Neither the woman's diligence, nor the reason
For the false dawns flickering behind them;
How in the old man's face all Egypt lay reflected;
Now could they see, through the enfolding cloth,
Now wide looked up the pearl eyes of the flying god.

2

HERMAN MOON'S HOURBOOK

Abasis

WALKING docile as you do down the empty street
The shadow-crowded granite, glow of sodium seas
It may shake the pavement under your feet
May drum with fists on air beside you
Mirage at your back may corrupt the clarity before you
May knock on your door when guests have turned and gone
May trouble your dream in the house (angel or monster
Figures recoil then into the cavity of the dream)
Dissolving bastions you had made sure were solid
Dispensing the life that is casual (not good but average)
May issue a spectre out of the throat of morning
Mask of sweat at noon
Forbidding the ecstasy that rides the noon's brow
Perplexing the cool that lays the dust at evening
Hollowing the tranced hill where you squat at sundown

Happy with friends to watch the turning of the stars

The Ant Sun

THE ant sun rams
Its ivory egg.
Grinding gears
Mix: it trundles on.
Slow river loomed,
A barge bellows;
Exhaust oils
Banked cloud of stone.

Sleep and waking
Swop lefts:
Old men, tenderly,
Thrump their brides
Of decades gone:
For white robes
They wait and stew,
The crowding misty girls.

And a day comes
And a day comes
With brisk birds.
A swab slops
Over dud marble.
Harder day comes
(Purity. Purity!)
With sweetly reeking coins.

The Forenoon

All the long forenoon, the loitering of insects;
Their invisible wings, whirring in choir and alley,
By lemon pyramids, in domes of organpounded air,
Over golden loaves that cool on glass in Greek Street.

One has flown to the vine slopes of a gated city,
One is crushed in a tube; one is a foreign king,
Stern in his carriage, popular, waving;
One with a whip stumbled after office girls,
And woke smiling. In iron shade
To one on a bench his nostril's curlew pipings bring
Concomitant visions of vacant moors.
One has dwelled among the springs and heard
A throbbing in the ark above their mountain.
One sidesteps a banker with a beak
And a dead baby dangling on a string from it.
One wisecracks. One darts giggling under a hat,
To munch a matchstick. One reads words
ARBOGAST FACTION PACT BUT HEAT RISES

One: severed from the great root the strong shrivel
One: the voluminous black fire answers their cry of terror
One: the plumed waves have burst long enough on this
shore
One: scattering the blind swarms that drink at the carcass.

The Dress

Her blue dress lightly
Is all my care.
Nothing I am
When not beside her.
Not every day,
Not any hour she passes,
Not always when she passes
Am I enough eager.

Not enough the streetcorner,
Nor the quiet room,
To take her body in.
Not enough the colour
Of patience, of murder
To draw her down
From the balcony she leans upon,
Highcrowned

And in the nighttime turned
Pale into amber over arch,
Inviolate sun.
Not enough the table
Under the awning, nor the elbow
Moving for me to see her,
For she must come
Unseen, without wanting:

Then I shall lightly
With all my care
Have my hand under
Her blue dress when she is there.

The Greenfly

I AM in the train. It is a summer afternoon.
I am in the corridor. A bar of warm aluminium
Cools my palms. The greenfly on the window
Is making an effort to move across the glass.

But six legs each with a claw at the end of it
And each claw groping in turn while the other five
Try to grip—but two feelers fencing with air—
But two tiny trellis wings of brinded fire—
It's not much help to a greenfly on a pane of glass.

Between me and the ruined plots rushing past,
Between me and the new blocks and dumps of brick,
Between me and several consecutive cranes
Fencing with air, clawed to earth, the roofs and halts,
This greenfly is an inquisitor.

You'll eat my one or two roses, is what I think.
Mine or someone else's. Some evenings I squirt
Swarms of your kind with a reliable poison.
Here it may not be the same. Here you are a most ravishing
Insect. Your six legs—they take the breath away.

No, here it is different. But what can I do?
We are rushing toward some constellation, so they say,
Onhurled by bricks and poisons, claws to grope and probe,
Gardens that contain a rose or two with any luck,
And I have no notion what to do about the killing now;
I have no notion why it starts, how it can end.

The Sniff

BEAK nose, bug eyes, almost bald head,
Drumskin over cheekbones, drawn in slack,
Wry over jawbones, flesh sucked into a mouth
Where pursed lips poise, to spit out evil taste,
He sniffs, with skidding jaw, and nose pinched,
Gills rise, then fall, and then he sniffs again,
Coughs up such snot as dropped back in his throat,
Till nostrils gaze again, eyesockets empty, and disclose
Darkness inside, where of small hairs undergrowths
    glisten,
Tricked with the stinted light this economic café gives.
He sniffs regularly, ravenously, glaring about himself;
Not picking, not blowing, he sits and sniffs; perhaps
To dislodge some crumb derelict after a choked meal?
To dull memories of cooking he loved as a little child?
Or to shake off desire, roused in a fragrance wafted over,
So that swallowed lust mysteriously glides into the dew-
    drop?

A too hard sniff culminates in a sly gurk.

Ode, on Contemplating Clapham Junction

ALL day rain fell. Morning:
one dusky liquid nymphless cave.

By noon the cave was crammed with ocean.
Two trains, full tilt, great whistling mackerel,
raced in an X under whale-shaped shadow.

Umbrellas, propped in halls, by tea,
behaved across the floor, like puppies.

All fall, by day, had rained. As late
as nine now moist sun
ushers a fearful agitation in

through curtains after lifting curtain.
Some thrush or other aches to sing.

Joy. One thrush. One overhasty . . .? No.
The sun mistaken, rising upside down?
Washed clean, no, space begins, unfolding

a million brilliant swishing fans
of bluish nothing.

Draughts of tomorrow
drawn slow
into empty lungs.

Tenebrae

ENTER my discourse as you dared and stood
Between your doorway and the dark and easily
The halflight curled into the hood of your hair.

Then you might have been
Other than what is ordinarily shown.

Shaking the timbers of the compatible world
Wisdom along her veins and her eyes withdrawn
One instant from her dream on the obedient stair,
Night seas unfurled through glory into her form.

Now among flaring things, now moving in the mist,
Their element in distress, might they not
Might they not have drowned in error for tenderness?

No fragrance fell, no motion troubled the air.
Back and gone in thickets of unbreakable glass,
Large-eyed, upright, indubitably gone she has.

This might have happened long, very long ago.

Waterloo Bridge

The rolled umbrella on my wrist,
How much air, crushed in the folds,
Aches for expulsion? What is starved,
Between my hat's crown and my own,
Of angering freshness deep deep down?

Chimney and sailor, ship and star,
Strangely belong. The cobbled lanes
Rib the long river; wet flint mounds
Tug at its roots; and cranes that inch
Athwart thick roofs, suppose this freedom.

Horns blast the ear, like anchors flung
By fluke through sludge to block
Derision riding seaward with the sun.
A meal of rats, doled out by love,—
Crushed by the silence, bolt it down.

Pointed Boots

At three in the morning,
A quietness descends on central railway stations.

A mail van, or an ambulance, may be there;
A man in pointed boots, a Miss Carew.

Quietness keeps them apart,
The quietness that descends on central railway
    stations.

It is not meant for me.
It is not meant for you.

3

Male Torso

BEFORE I woke, the customed thews
Alighted on strangeness.
Crammed over booms of vine,
The once buxom canvas quilled.

From his hot nest, before I woke,
The snowgoose flew, in skyward rings;
And funnelled air that filled my mouth
Rang with his wingbeat.

The customed eyes, before I woke, were glass;
A bleating queen whose legs were sheaths
Of hammered moon fed swill to pigs;
With needle oars they swept her bark

Through floes of starfruit, dolphins cutting
Under her eyelid's bow blue arcs in air;
And the beat of their oars like drums
Fanned my hushabye head.

Before I woke, no savour was;
But three birds sang that song they piped as girls,
Of sweetness, golden-rinded, and the fountaintree,
For mortal grapes cooled in my hands.

Then down the quartz-walled galleries of ears I coiled,
Before I woke; cymbals clashing sliced their hill,
And there with bulls my skew-wigged mother trod
Her crocus dance around its axle;

Counterwheeling Horn and Bear
Shared in her coronal the thud of fingertips on flutes,
Until my customed silence dipped and rose,
And gall was mine and darkness was.

I live now in a hutch of mud,
Without a floor, nailed by the sun,
Now for the interminable writhing sea
A fair food housed in roofless marble.

But if I wake to sniff the air of clustered stars,
I'm clothed in dew, for babes to drink,
The snowgoose moors her nest on light,
And the small horned worms walk high with hope.

Southern Electric Teddygirl

POLITER
And less dull than I, gazing,
Since ribs which mackintosh plates
(Belt on the ninth hole) must make,
For ease, one vertical
Brief tube, topped by a face
Eye-staring at a moon—
So Pomona, worn thin by fish and comics,
Hair yet
Bushes of torchlight
Bounding over hills through whose glades
Cool surf burrows—
Here knees and nose going
No particular way
Back, insistent, toward
Algae, plasm in pools that Pomona inched
Her million years from, now
Leaning back, on springs,
She peers for huts flash by,
Blinks with blued condescending
Eyelids over roof seas
And yellow skies that roar,
Recrossing the ankles
Her winkle-pickers bruise, to resume
Into Orpington
Her airy trail.

Amiel

I WAS a myriad dark sad Swiss philosopher;
my window slid by pool upon rock pool
of stockstill foreign things. Unthrift imagination
sent ventilating zephyrs down, not reckoning, alas,
they would consume those sunken plants that coigned
and caverned out my vision. White
terrified women picked up their skirts and ran.
Fat pedestrians overheard
my elegant unabating monotone as they plodded past.
It meant nothing. The lake, how still.

Travelled a little,—in a tight spread
from thin roots I clung to like a madman.
But my world—it was migration without end,
hunting that civil queen, through crags of glass—
Frigia, Cymia, Delphica, Chimeria—
some world: a candid music, drained of green,
and the sky unthumbed as that unageing dreadful flesh
my brackish beard
at moments anchored kisses in. Rain falling
enhaloed echoing fanshapes far over the lake,
to pit its drumskin.

Then perhaps I knew
alluring hope gobbles the stubborn brain
as insect insect. Ultimately though,
nature concerned me only somewhat. Constancy
was what I wanted. Constancy. With nothing to yield it,
least of all Amiel. Known beauty made
for vacant stares and sudden rages; bred familiarity
with the steeplejack's dread of the long drop, hunched
howling into the myriad dark neat nature mimes
with her fossil mask. And the gull's
blue glide, to come by that, but how?

And the lake beaten flat as Heine's nightingales;
white the remembered shore alone, the torrent green,
a green hunger, hoarding the celestial!

Was pathos winged, I wonder, even in the provinces?
When they have danced their fullness into hers
and drop, before her image quickens, moves
mysterious beyond horror where they moved,
does Europe weep harsh vengeance for her sons?
I toiled on, treading that emptiness. Forgotten April
found me at last, gasping among the wardrobes and azaleas,
the shrunken hand still writing, writing,
the vague soul dwarfed already by the asphodels.

Absences

On either down a wreath of plume
Carved clear on the hill, her spent
Body aroused in a cedar dream,
She lay the warm day long,
And there a wraith he lay.

Their feathers swim as each breathes
Undone by slumber, and half-askance
They stare away to the other eyes:
They see nought of the night,
Though an emerald semblance outward goes.

A double sleep uncovers them,
Body abounding, drowned now,
And the stiff limbs athwart the sands
Hollow the light their glow gives up:
Entwining lie, nor drowsing doubt
Though time divides, the earth amends.

On neither one the wild grows,
No wheaten acres wave their smile,
No bramble on their ankle is:
For whole is the body if spent at all,
Just as she lay the day long,
And he a wraith beside.

China Shop Vigil

USEFUL these bowls may be;
what fatness makes the hollows glow,
their shadows bossed and plump.

Precisely there a wheel whirling backward
flattens them. Knuckles whiten on copper:
headless men are hammering drums.

Cup and teapot may be such comforters:
small jaws mincing chatter
over the bad blood between us once.

When baking began, the air in jugs frothed
for milk, or lupins. Now mob is crushed
by mob, what fatness but in wild places,

where some half dozen dusty mindful men
drinking from gourd or canvas huddle,
and can speak at last of the good rain.

Nightlabourer

FOR GUY DAVENPORT

RECLINED the body of the world:
No hill whiter with olive,
Hair burned gold by the sun,
Target of fair skin,
Head of a traveller, to pity turned,
With kingcurled hair and hat of fire,
Pity upon the near hill,
With roseate staff and silver shoon,
Brown body, bent like a sail,
Shoulders bound to the treesap:

Now pity will suffer of love,
Yet dries its acreage to a chart
Where crouched the leopard sings,
No watercourses move;
Will bless the leopard for his thirst,
No tempter offering
Cavebearded king or saint
No fruit more gold than his encircled head:

No hill whiter with olive:
Will watch on,
Though the night fall,
Will to the earth his suppliance commit,
As head bows to the knee,
Body curls in the hill,
Leopard kneels in the end at the gate of the city:

For though the thorn
Press needles through his palm,
Pity too near is entered still unseen:
Beast, curltongued at the cave's mouth,
But to the head laid down under the hill,
To the eye, brushed by sleep's silken sleeve,

Will bring the light the leopard watches by
So that the olive springs from his blood's overcast
And seeds ring the bright blind bone:
No sail, no land, more curled in amethyst
Than pity's silence in the stone,
Than the grave hair risen to a golden country.

Rhododendron Estranged in Twilight

'Und kommen muss zum heil'gen Ort das Wilde
Von Enden fern . . .'

Hölderlin, *Friedensfeier*

IT crests this tunnelled London hill,
Growing a little space behind this house.
It stands aloof. It is contained by calm.

A blaze of bloom in May now, no hunched bush,
Gawky it is, and stands as in deep water
With slender boles akimbo, coral horned;
Then mutely swayed by undulating wind.

Sky's porcelain inclines, unplaceable,
For each taut cave of flame a shifting margin.
Roots rustle underground, make arch advances.
Red grows oblivious, fat, on eating shade.

Air sweetly rinsing it, the image floats
Into its own reflection imperceptibly.
A slotted mask with one mind's eye divines

Through emerald tropic, ruthless dream,
Lust at meridian, unclenched energy rising:
The sylvan slattern, bawd bedaubed with flesh
Drawn off some lurching drunkard's feline whim,

Green windgod of the hill in hot pursuit,
Those olive shoulders, wrenched back, risking all,
Then, unresisting, thighs from bark unsheathed.

Yet nature's needle teeth bite off what wrong
Reflection cries in them. Quicksilvered man,
Turn you estranged to risk unbaffled more:

This rose unfolding in the air's clear volume
Scents out its own lost womb of origin.
The shown form whispers of the invisible one.
The hill's firm headstone marks the shrine this was.

Without Shoes

'. . . unbeschuht.' Mörike, *Peregrina.*

ONE goes lightly
   down ignorant rays
across history buoyant
   with fruit and shade

One goes lightly
   mother and father wave
from dormer windows
   of the dove-starred house

Happy anthems—
   owls make naked
women laugh
   in the dark orchard

Babies chirping
   girls of cork
and moonboys quiver
   nailed by the bowstring

Perhaps an orange
   tastes of Padua
an alien chord
   spits visions

But one goes lightly
   over echo-dancing shores
up wrinkled lightning
   surges a friend

yielding tombs of air to trumpet wings
   along whose colonnade
without shoes
   one goes lightly.

News From Norwood

PROFESSOR Palamedes darts down Westow Street.
Nothing explains how he avoids
Colliding with mutton, plastics, pianos.
Professor Palamedes, darting down Westow Street,
Tunnels through petrol fumes and tundra;
Rhomboid oysterbeds under his rubbers,
Sparrows and sandwiches scatter before him.

Where is he going, Professor Palamedes?
It's well past three. What has he forgotten?
What can he have forgotten, Professor Palamedes,
Who stood with Agur by Solomon's elbow,
Who flogged the sea, full of nymphs and sheep,
Whom meat moods or helpful harmonies do not perplex?

Let us say he is going toward the stranger.
Again: he is going toward the stranger.
No matter who. The stranger. Who showed his face.
Who showed his face over Solomon's shoulder;
Who saw at Salamis, as planks buckled and the nymphs
Cheered, how sheep just went on cropping grass,
Side by side, to a tinkling of bells.

Paganini

CEILINGS of knobbed gold
almost flew apart;
glass pagoda chandeliers
rocked as thousands
of frilled palms
hammered in pairs,
for he paused—the rosewood
shrank to a gutted box,
with inky date and name
on a label inside.

Urchin and cat, before dawn,
heard heavenly scratchings,
underground, as they ran
for oven and fish.
Horrible cries
under the grill!
From a cellar little evidenced
by the one candle,
came shrieks to appal
the running thief.

Matutinal Adventures of a Third Person Illustrating the Untold Agony of Habit

ANACHRONIST or no, he was not one
  to disregard for long the unhurt daffodils'
rosarium, chrysanthos, quills
  plucked from the prancing porcupine sun
their holy circle slew. And soon, as though
  in nature metaphor now faced a match,
rounding his periplum arose
  a second sanctum: snowblue dorsum of nuthatch
winding a six-clawed wedge of sky up a hawthorn put
  a knife like brightness through his eyeball, moderate
as bodies flighted perfect to their purpose.

  How come then so soon the immortal had forsaken
its habitat on this last holy London hill?
  Some scrubbing housewife, had she put them wise,
who had been angels in the suburban sunrise?
  Or had six hundred intervening heartbeats shaken
the three directions time can choose to travel
  into one crooked labyrinthine shadow?
For on his countermarch he found them gone,
  found them, but only found them flower and bird.
So brushed his hair at home, then ate his bacon
  with the air of a being invisibly injured,
yet strangely relieved not to have to be saying so.

Cadgwith: 6 PM +

ALTERNATE light and shade englobe
the chimneyed hill. Silver shafts slip
mute under heaven's rib, and open bars.

Four cardinals astride the public bench
dip their noses deep in the grogpots.

Gulls wheel clear,
to skirt the corpus mysticum flung taut
in ribbed gold from swart cliff to winged horizon.

Bloodshot
the venerable sea shifts
one drunkard eye, and wipes its white moustaches.

Gulls turn on their heel.
Night blots the conqueror out.

Climbing a Pebble

WHAT did it mean (I ask myself), to climb a pebble.
From the head of a boy depends a very thin cloud.
A red speck shifting on the Roman Campagna.
This sea-rubbed pebble has no cleft for toes.

It is simple, the ant said (my Nares and Keats).
You start low down, with caution. You need not
Slash your soles for lime like medieval Swiss.
No, but with spread arms, easing up, imperceptibly
Colluding with the air's inverted avalanche.
This cushions, O, the aching spine.

A very thin cloud is falling from the sky.
A shot, a shifting robe of crimson,
Whiffs of powder on the wind—
The sidelong buffet slams. And still you cling,
Still easing upward; giant glades, they creaked and shone,
Fresh mown, now small below—you do not smell them.

And you begin to know what it can mean,
Climbing a pebble. The paradise bird
Drops, dies, with beak fixed in the ground.
An urchin made off with its cloudthin tail.
A cardinal, with footmen to load his fowling pieces,
Peppers Italian larks a glass held spellbound.

The glass was tied to an owl, the owl to a stick.
I struck the pebble, digging, as the sun went up.

The Lake of Thun

NUDE forms of inshore bathers bend
like shafts of light across the lake.

Fruitful the bones man-dreamers bind
with mind and bitterness, yet rock

Between these clefts of flesh from sense
cloud ordures now, blue innocence.

Flames also blue, through liquid smoke,
flounce overhead, each clay-expired:

Local exhaustions throb, the yachts
expand amidships, curving past

Kingfisher fleet. Three falter, lost,
white throats untaut, stabbed by the wind:

Plunge of this poised knife caught, he bled
who here chose friends, broke here his bread.

Thinking of Hölderlin

(HILLS NEAR HEIDELBERG)

NEVER mind avarice; the hills
squander at least a sprawl
of steep oak. Speak
of the moroccan green
pines that fetlock them; of rumps,
rutted by axes; of bristling stung flanks,
flushed by puffs of cloud—

for first and last
who saw them crammed the air
with hawk and temple;
and what fetched them avarice, in the interim,
cannot change their green
bulk and butts of sandstone,
let alone rot the wits, killing,

as hawk and temple, his, for the crime
of being put, by them, wise to the least thing.
No, not in his name
do I join these crooked words, lest I miss
for him, more than temple, his hawk,
now lofted by their hot gusts, now
plucking the crowded vermin from their folds.

Antiphon, After Laforgue's Stérilités

THERE torridest lagoons decant
  steeple cool and star
in jugs ophelian orphans drain
  haunting springs
  with oh and ah
  in father-want
  in mother-pain.

Coagular cloacal jig
  the cicatrice
feline ophelias christen itch—
  it robes the gnat
  in candle grease,
  it hogs the fat
  in fuller fig.

An oval-torsoed swan we saw
  furrowing air
and the air shook and clung for joy;
  that duple egg
  we swallowed raw,
  routed for Troy,
  her shambling dead.

What phantoms reign when gods ascend
  our haunted springs?
Quaffers of cloud, we do not know
  ah from an oh
  nor a nailed hand
  from fists of blood
  lambasting things.

Then if a wise Ophelia found
  tarantular
the moon domain, its milken hills
  a serpent ground,
  and chose to shun,
  shaken with tears,
  the dogged sun—

Her caryatid dream conjures
  (if dream it be)
ophelias more fool than she
  to prophylax
  against the swan
  in horizon-
  tal parallax.

Occipital, precipitous
  though hungers drive
moonshine in schisms round the skull,
  no phantoms fuss
  their seraph lull
  from solar rose
  to honey hive.

And man, misty history man, for all that,
  identifies
his shadowshapes with seraphim.
  The garb of him!
  And hopes disguise,
  ellipsoid, slim,
  a Cheshire Cat—

Kedge-anchored in the axletree
(immortal moon
feline ophelias catechize)
mortally afraid
of being free
from once and soon
from whats and whys.

A bubble moon we saw, we saw
a cloven tree;
and phantoms thronged the threshingfloor
and orphans came
and did not dance.
Eyeless, and lame,
they did not dance.

There too we heard the dew's descent
on acid hills
and shade elide with sliding shade:
what image made
them so lament,
sobbing through space,
that were innocent?

Glaucus

1

ALONG the grass I saw the sun creep scything shade,
Blue fin flickering under water grazed my head.
A fine blade shivering bled my thought, alas:
The silent reaper comes, not asking who.

I saw in a cloudless kingdom under the sea
A lean man with flesh of light walking, fearing none.
Under the tree, upright, a sunlit lady stood:
Thunder sang, unbowed a branch hung green.

Along the grass I on this other earth again
Let my fingers glide, now I delight to touch
Plain things, things hungry and forlorn, that pass.
Born in the lightning, they hide their birth.

2

MISERABLE in my meandering
Round wreathed weeds and green seawater sounds,
I had seen her shadow on the water.

There was her stillness I sought after.

Who, when I touched her hands,
To cover my memory of a music
And singing still half submarine, who woke me?

Riding mystery in a blaze of miracle,
We rose to peace. But I have left her now;
I feed on shells, I drink dereliction.

Then was she lost? Yet sometimes,
Warning from space my songs,
Her visitations trace beyond recall
And with simplicity all I have done.

3

NIGHTFALLS have known, nightrisings not neglected
These, our trunks entwined with the veins' blue branches,
For the roof flowered there and forked above us,
Trellised spring abounded beneath us,
And if the rubble walls reckoned on starlight, any,
No hooded void of dream lay down between us.
Shadow and blood, we dropped, hovered,
Dry or wet, wrestled with ardour, flame spurted,
Vine sprang heavenward, with gold streams arching,
Earth had no way, no wish to hinder it; the harvest
Fields were afire, we reaped them, from mouths of the dead
Riper the stooks rose, swifter the seas ran on,
Till the pain of living came sweeter for sunrise.
What heaven's tongue, at dawn, had tasted us?
When you woke up, one tangle of eyes and hair,
You squirmed for the delight of it, your hot breasts
Suddenly cold, you smiled, into dark we plunged,
Rose again in a flash of angel, so that the kissed skin
Shivered, grasped at us, so that we moved
Yet could not move, outstripped, alone, we clung
To what we had, the stillness, pitying each,
Each pitiless drinking.
Now crabbed days come,
I think of the skin's hillcrests, kingdoms where we
glimpsed
A simple sun, as through the eye of a needle.
Thirst made us rich then, but now the thread draws thin.
Knit in the fire, our gilded shadows dwindle.
Do not forget the little significant things, for it is known
We may unravel when this winter comes.

The King of the Chaldees

(*II Chronicles 36 : 17*)

BLACK food for the stranger at the door, who did not knock.
The burnt clay does not mind a mouthful of blood.
In a narrow street, far in the sun, by ancient anchors,
Many women sat and stitched, all one cool afternoon.

Ashes for the hunger man, trapped beneath roof beams.
Fresh nettles hardly notice him. The ruined apes
Who stalk that street are shod in robbed old shoes of his.

Some shining thing twisted across the dark shaft's floor.
There is blackberry. The crunch of walled sea desists.
Torpedoes crowd through fastidious reefs of thorn
At one touch. They hammer the fronds with quick cries.

The tiny arm did not reach that far down, or want
Profit and loss. Music mounting from the shut room
Made larger fear and the tall mother tremble.

Now the brown river heaves with thumping hulls,
And the first buoys dong as it swarms to their chains.
And it does not mind the drag of tides when it enters their
grip;
Nor can the salt forced down its fishy throat make much odds.

Thirst

SHOULD wine and melon, jug and wasp
break from their images, their single sense
shine in the air, burn in the wind:
then were the ripe within grasp—
this axle of the mind.

In cooler cisterns frogs decide to sing.
How morning sun
silvered their throats in your battered pail.
How long since the dragon heard, on waking,
your footstep, heavier, cross his hill.

The Lake of Zürich

(FOR ROBERT WALSER, SWISS POET, IN HIS MADNESS)

THAN sky, the lemon, dredged, more dark this liquid.
Fluminal violet, in a lockjaw littoral, swings
Wind-swathed, wind-cradled.

Asunder the scooped rays
With fanged spire sentinels at last unbend
Over slender moles, where pedalos are harnessed.

Dazed, mad or dumb unscented gaze, but ladies
Emit, by twos and threes, conspicuous shadows
In a suave star-acre, hum in the voids they leave.

Sickle through throats of cloud the moon drops rustling
Down, as for a day forgotten. Configures heaven,
Curved luminous, in concord, over this brain's trim bed.

Loll, where the rat stalks, the gowned fish and breed.

Air glabrous, may taste of acid, beast uncoil
Cocked like an abandoned eyebrow over
All ease, dark arbour, armoured there, his tail.

Time runs thick as thieves this iron way of water.

Art Machine

(the automatically rotating epidiascope at the
exhibition of Brazilian art, Paris 1960)

THERE are needles lancing disks
a saint soared across a crowd
I saw tormented women
whirl down a tall hill
a prairie lobster
polyps in a wedge and bronze
twin birds that claw their combs
then boots with sieves in black pools

of beams and winds
the silver fruit

harpoons have been plunged
through grinding millstones
Saint Paul shook his fist
at packed cafés
three pairs of trousers
float from a window
being women whose
rumps must weigh tons

in rice fields
negroes prowl

as shadows ooze from hills
horn pincers wrung
quit their cactus paternoster
plasm flashing wings
a nude candelabra
tilts the tricorn
to allure at that angle as
her image pounces

negroes prowl
in rice fields
rinsing silver fruit
of beams and winds

Intrusions

ON rare mornings
  a man at my table
gazes into the left-hand sun.
  Huge heat arriving
snuffles glass and bars, against
  his doubtless smile.

Seas come crashing, horned waves
  airing their volume;
bull-roarers
  make brave men tremble; pitch
flops on gorgon shields as yelping
  gnomes flit batlike by
through cactus stars to holy laughter.

I stand on the threshold, barefoot;
  boosted by half a plank, having guessed
its place by rule of suns,
  as on some thick fly throng
a bone Electra, royally gaoled,
  I print my footmark.

It is a room
  of rod and exit; taller weeds
dry in the jar on a plinth of blue.
  Yet not in fear
this lone loon starts on my intrusion,
  waves in vacancy, with dwindling
hands held to an old old friend.

Metropolitan Oratory

'Thy hand, great Anarch!', *Dunciad*

(When the sleeve of Asia detonates the silence,
Curtains are torn apart, the amphitheatre darkens)

Stream out of underground in piston postures,
Fistful of icicles, bicycles, electric dancers,
Bronze walls, stations of curved glass, peristyles:
Here terminate the long-rehearsed migrations;
Here acrobats, upright in the catafalque,
Spring to volcanic voltage, blossom and overflow
In blood diagrams for the boom of the hospitals.
Here germinates such August flight to the sea
That the gold horde gathers on a million horses,
Dragon diagonals into the shade of the pyramid;
And where the stone wings ejaculate spectres of future,
Here are the living the havoc of all the dead.

(There is a garden, white with rubber flowers,
Where lover male with lover female goes)

Stone, oil, pedestals, black stone pitched
Into the floodlit dock where the deadwork rears,
And into dust and thorns moulded to throat height
Re-echo divinations of the body that never was,
Bouquets of steel for caesarean entrances,
Pallor for widowed insects at their industries.

Where overtime recoils from midnight onward,
Here is the blind beast intimate with the defeated;
Then out of fractured jaws eruct in fountains
Acres of eyes and iron parabolas:
Therefore the dawn blonde of office will circumvent
The purple and gold pool spilled on the pavement.

(Spires, brass, pyramid, pistons
Plunge as Arcturus' convoys pass beyond.)

Five Psalms of Common Man

'Je n'aime pas le dimanche'

1

WHISKY whipping g-string Jaguar megaton
sometimes a 'purely rational human being'

it's me they tell of yonder sea devoid of amber
it's me they tell of column and haunting song

noncommittal me my mumble eaten
by the explosions of clocks and winds without routine

not fountains not millennia of light inextinguishable
ebbing through column and throat with its
    wombwombwomb

come my pet my demagogue excruciate me watching
yonder fountain douse the yolky dunes

2

THE creatures of coal have looked for you all over;
the creatures of tea heard a snatch of song, it was not you.

The creatures of smoke have looked for you all over;
the creatures of tar saw a tree, it was not you.

The hand was not you, nor the hairy ear;
the belly was not you, nor the anklebone.

The eyeball was not you. Tongue and teeth
and jawbone were not you. The creatures of hair

have looked for you all over; the creatures of snow
touched a locked door, it was not you.

The creatures of paper have looked for you all over;
the creatures of steel smelled thick wallets, it was not you.

These creatures wanted to be free to look for you;
and all the time you looked to be free of their want for you.

3

W. N. P. Barbellion (pseudonymous)
March 1915
sees 'on the top of an empty omnibus
a little heap of dirty used-up bus tickets
collected by chance in the corner'

felt sick
the number of persons
the number of miles
the number of buses

at all times
the number of voices
the number of voices not speaking to one another
perplexity without surprise

Avenues Madison Shaftesbury Opéra
the number of heart beats
without number

the sick one is he on whom his desire advances asking
why
the sick one is he who has begun all over again
not waiting not
'waiting that hour which ripens to their doom'

he speaks (Adolf Eichmann April 1961)
'in starchy, clerkish language
full of abstractions
pedantry
euphemism'

4

MY blind wife kicking in her flesh of flies.
My blind wife in her ring of ribs beating me flat.
But no shard of keg shall cool my last bones.

The flies were dancing in their ring.
Their ring was dancing in the flies.
The ring desired by the nature of flies.

Stomach eyes packing it all in tight.
Knotted wings kicking in a glue film.
Ghosted in glue was the nature of eyes.

Revolt severe if sieved for its ghost of motive.
Air without motive rubbing in the arid throat.
My blind wife I warm to the coolness of bones.

5

ORDER imagined against fear is not order.
Saith man. Fear imagined against order
only negates or does not negate existing order.
Out of a rumbling of hollows an order is born
to negate another existing order of fear.

Nights broken before they end, interrupting
the millennia of my vigilance, saith man.
The nights of past time never slept to the end
re-enact themselves in the existing order of fear.

Another order of fear is chaos.
Images of chaos variously coordinated
by disparate imaginations accord or do not accord
to their seasons in time enacting the indeterminations.
The orders revolve in the ring or do not evolve.

The orders revolve as improvisations against fear,
changed images of chaos. Without fear, nothing.
Let me, saith man, take another look at the sea again.
And in his ear begin the rumblings of keels again.